One Spring Day

Original edition published in Japan by
Shiko Sha Company, Ltd., Tokyo, Japan, 1977
© 1977 Shiko Sha Company Ltd.

Published in the U.S.A. in 1979 by Judson Press, Valley Forge, PA 19481

Printed in Japan

ISBN 0-8170-0821-7

The name JUDSON PRESS is registered as a trademark in the U.S. Patent
Office.

One Spring Day

By Shigeko Yano
English text by Yukiko Kawakami

Judson Press ® Valley Forge

From here I cannot see what is over the hill.

But I know that there is a green meadow.

And many sheep are there.
I will see them when I walk to the meadow.

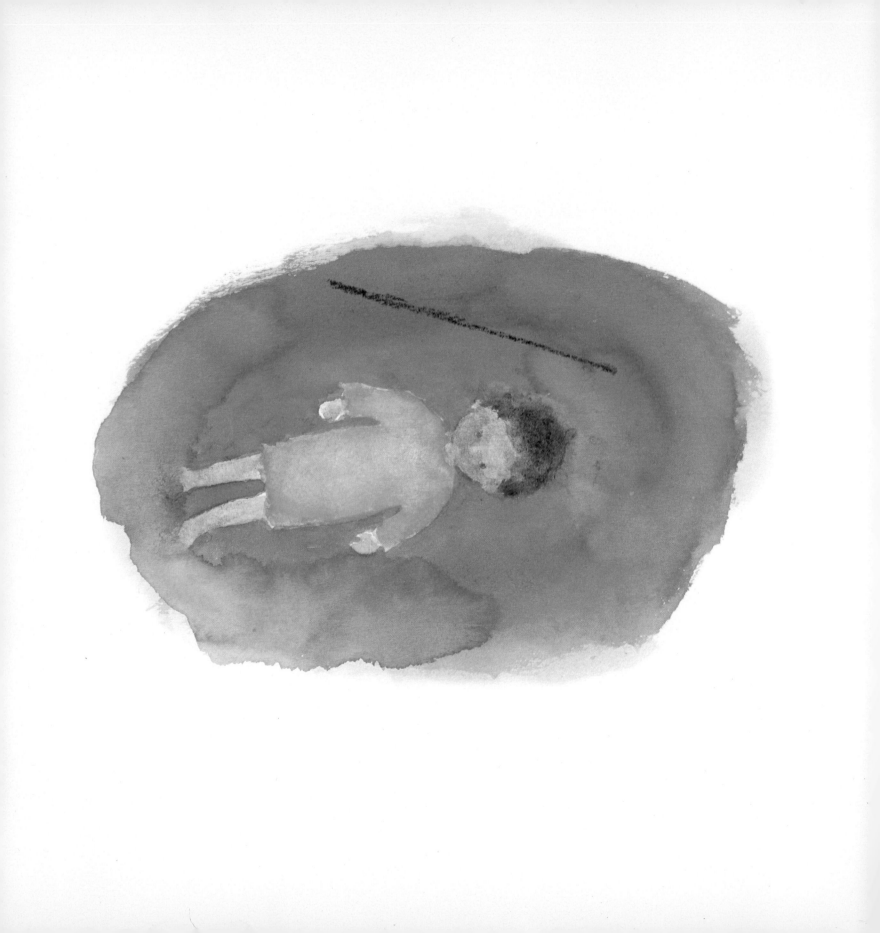

I lie down in the green grass and look up.
I see the blue sky.
The sun is shining in the blue sky.
But I do not see the stars when it is day.

Sometimes at night I can see many stars
   and the moon.
I cannot see all of the stars in the sky,

but they are there.

The deep forest lies beyond the meadow.
I can see the forest,
but I cannot see all the trees and the flowers.

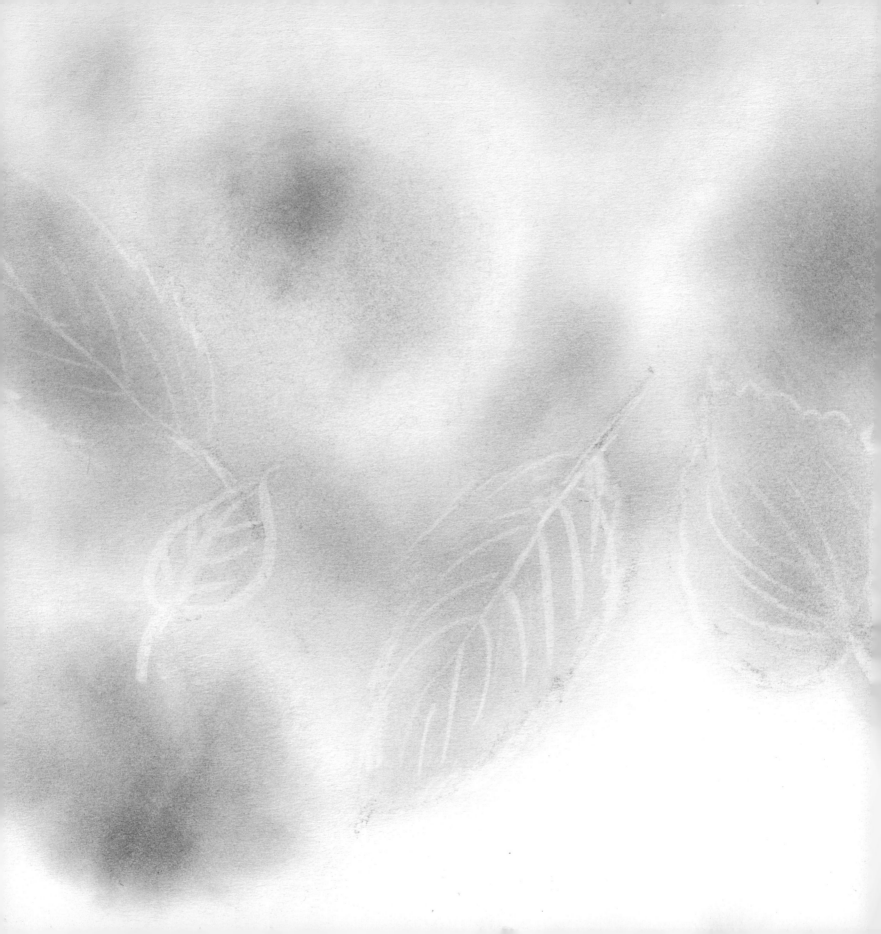

But they are there,
waiting for the new baby birds' visit.

I cannot see the new baby birds in the nest.
The new baby birds are asleep in the eggs.
They are waiting until it is time for them to come out.
I cannot see them, but they are there.

Some day they will have beautiful wings,
and they will sing pretty songs.

I do not see my house in the sunset,
but I know that it is there.

I cannot see my mother.
I cannot see my father.

But I will see them when I go home.

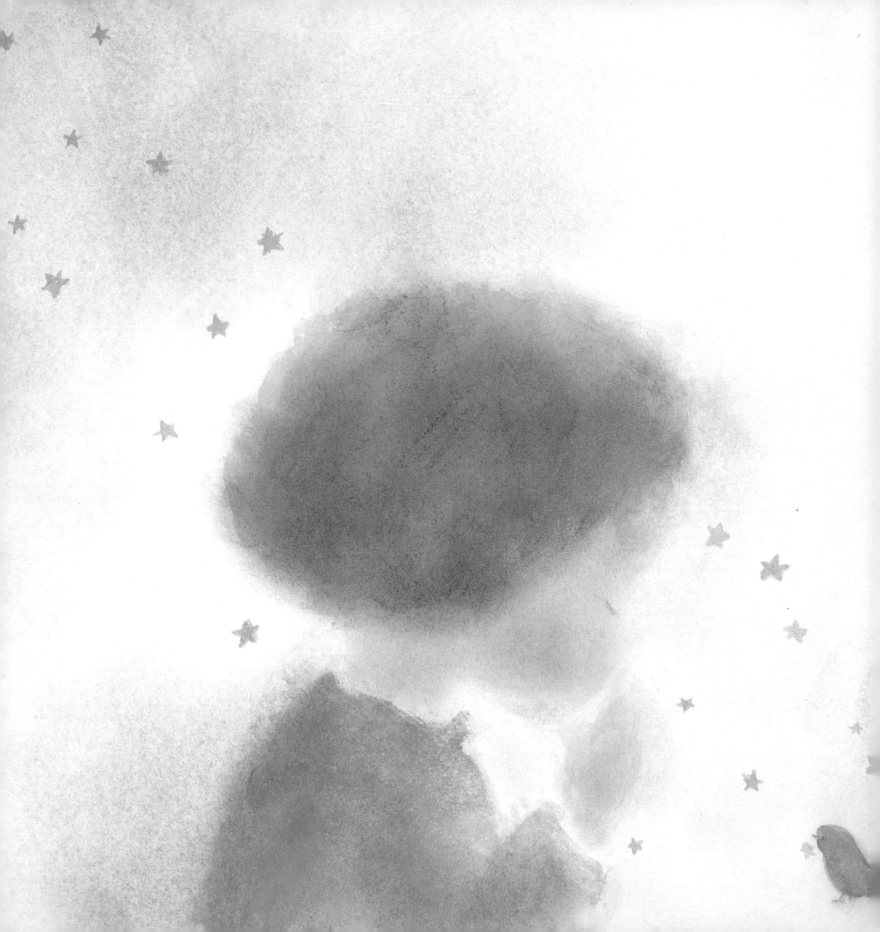

In bed I close my eyes.
Then I can see the birds, the sheep, the flowers,
    the trees, the stars, and the moon.
But some things I can never see.

I cannot see the song of a bird,
    but the bird sings.
I cannot see the smell of a flower,
    but I can smell the flower.
I cannot see the warmth of the sheep,
    but I can touch the sheep.

I cannot see God who created the earth.
But I know that God is there!